Effective Supervisory Skill Building
Study Guide

By Christine Becker

A study guide to accompany the book

Effective Supervisory Practices:
***Better Results Through Teamwork*, Fifth Edition**

ICMA
PRESS

ICMA advances professional local government worldwide. Its mission is to create excellence in local governance by developing and advancing professional management of local government. ICMA, the International City/County Management Association, provides member support; publications, data, and information; peer and results-oriented assistance; and training and professional development to more than 9,000 city, town, and county experts and other individuals and organizations throughout the world. The management decisions made by ICMA's members affect 185 million individuals living in thousands of communities, from small villages and towns to large metropolitan areas.

Printed in the United States of America

CONTENTS

About the Author

Christine Becker is president, Christine Becker Associates, Washington, D.C., and formerly director of training with ICMA and deputy executive director with the National League of Cities.

Select ICMA Books

A Budgeting Guide for Local Government, Second Edition

Citizen Surveys for Local Government: A Comprehensive Guide to Making Them Matter, Third Edition

The Effective Local Government Manager, Third Edition

Effective Supervisory Practices: Better Results Through Teamwork, Fifth Edition

The Ethics Edge, Second Edition

Human Resource Management in Local Government: An Essential Guide, Third Edition

Leading Performance Management in Local Government

Local Government Police Management, Fourth Edition

Management Policies in Local Government Finance, Sixth Edition

Managing Fire and Emergency Services

Service Contracting: A Local Government Guide, Second Edition

Strategic Planning for Local Government, Second Edition

COURSE OVERVIEW

The *Effective Supervisory Skill Building Study Guide* provides review questions, worksheets, and learning activities to supplement the concepts and practices covered in the fifth edition of *Effective Supervisory Practices: Better Results Through Teamwork,* also published by ICMA. Together the study guide and book comprise what we call the "course." The course is designed to help both new and experienced supervisors become more skilled and successful at their jobs. It offers a framework for improving supervisory practices, supporting professional development, and ensuring high-quality public service.

The course is divided into sixteen lessons, each based on one chapter in the *Effective Supervisory Practices* book, and one final summary lesson designed to help plan for the future. The lessons are grouped into seven units to highlight major components of supervisory practice:

- Unit I: From Employee to Supervisor to Leader
- Unit II: Getting the Work Done
- Unit III: Developing Your Team
- Unit IV: Ensuring High Performance and Results
- Unit V: Managing the Workplace Environment
- Unit VI: Serving the Public
- Unit VII: Becoming a Successful Supervisor

The units offer opportunities for combining lessons to cover related material in one session and for adding supplemental, organization-specific materials and resources to maximize the learning experience. The final unit provides a lesson on action planning to help you summarize key learning points and identify action steps for future growth as a supervisor.

Course audience and objectives

This course is designed primarily for local government supervisors who want to enhance their skills, broaden their perspectives, and expand their supervisory and management capability. It can serve as both a *refresher* for experienced supervisors seeking to update their knowledge and sharpen their skills and an *introduction* for new supervisors just making the transition from peer to boss. In addition, it can provide a perspective on the skills needed to become a successful supervisor for employees who aspire to supervisory and management positions.

While the course is intended primarily for group training programs, the study guide and book can also be used by individuals and small groups of supervisors for self-learning.

Overall learning objectives for the *Effective Supervisory Practices Skill Building* course are to

- Broaden understanding of the roles and responsibilities of today's local government supervisors
- Connect theories of supervisory practice to real-life situations
- Encourage thoughtful discussion among practicing supervisors to increase learning
- Build confidence among supervisors by applying what you learn in the classroom to the day-to-day challenges you face on the job.

Lesson components

Each lesson in the study guide contains these elements:

- A learning objective describing what the lesson is designed to accomplish
- A reading assignment from the *Effective Supervisory Practices* book
- A summary of the chapter content and lesson focus
- Lesson outcomes that summarize concepts, ideas, and principles that you should be familiar with when you finish the lesson
- Review questions to check your understanding of the ideas in the chapter and provide a framework for discussion among supervisors about important practices both in class and on the job

- Learning activities to deepen your understanding of the content by connecting the chapter information to your specific organization
- A "Taking It Forward" section to help you apply specific skills and behaviors on the job, both to enhance your learning and make a difference in your work unit. Taking it forward involves identifying specific actions, such as introducing your work team to how values and ethics guide their work or leading a discussion on positive benefits of a performance evaluation process, trying out the actions, and then documenting the impact of your efforts.[1]

The study guide includes some worksheets that you can complete right in the book. For other activities, we recommend that you prepare separate worksheets and notes, whether on paper or electronically, for your personal use and for discussion with other members of your group.

When you begin the course, you should decide how to keep your learning materials organized—in a notebook, on an office computer system, or on a personal laptop, iPad, or other electronic device. Some organizations provide tools, resources, and file space on an employee intranet to support employees who are participating in a supervisory training course using these materials. Regardless of the tool you use, it is important to keep your course work organized for class discussions as well as for use on the job.

A word about differences

No two local governments are alike. The range of programs and services provided and the expectations of supervisors in helping to carry out those programs and deliver those services may vary considerably from the practices and examples covered in the book and the study guide. To account for these differences, the book and study guide offer a range of resources to accommodate different perspectives and different levels of expertise and sophistication. The goal is to provide a flexible learning experience that encourages supervisors to look for connections and apply learning to their situations.

---

[1] The "Taking It Forward" section is adapted from the Overland Park, Kansas, Development Pathways Supervisory program, designed by Pam Kisslinger, training and organization development coordinator in Overland Park, and is used in this study guide with permission.

1

Unit I:

FROM EMPLOYEE TO SUPERVISOR TO LEADER

This unit focuses on you as an individual supervisor. The lessons focus particularly on the transition from an individual employee who is responsible for specific tasks to a supervisor who guides the work of other employees to achieve work unit expectations and a leader who inspires employees, models ethical and values-based behavior, and draws on sources of influence to achieve work unit and organizational outcomes. Lessons in this unit are:

Lesson 1: Roles of a Supervisor

Lesson 2: Supervisory Leadership

Lesson 3: Ethics

Lesson 1:
ROLES OF A SUPERVISOR

Lesson objective:
To increase understanding of the broad role of the supervisor in today's environment.

Reading assignment:
Effective Supervisory Practices Fifth Edition, Chapter 1: Roles of a Supervisor

Lesson outcomes:
When you finish this lesson, you should

- Understand the major responsibilities of a supervisor and how those responsibilities relate to your job
- Be comfortable with the challenge of transitioning from peer to boss, if you are a new supervisor
- Know the value of delegation to your supervisory success and how to be an effective delegator
- Be familiar with the characteristics of a successful supervisor
- Know what you want to get out of this course.

Lesson overview

This lesson serves as an introduction to both the course and your roles as a local government supervisor. Chapter 1 of *Effective Supervisory Practices* highlights key roles of supervisors and identifies eight major supervisory practices that are keys to your success:

1. Understanding the difference between leading and managing
2. Moving from being a peer to being a supervisor
3. Building and sustaining a team
4. Involving employees in decision making
5. Delegating effectively
6. Identifying and resolving problems
7. Making jobs more interesting and rewarding
8. Building relationships.

Review questions

1. Drawing on the information in Chapter 1 and your experience, what are the most important supervisory responsibilities in your current position? How are the supervisory responsibilities you identified similar to and different from the responsibilities listed on pages 3 to 4 of the book chapter?
2. What is the difference between leading and managing?
3. If you are a new supervisor, what action steps can you take to move from being one of the gang to the person in charge? If you are an experienced supervisor, what steps did you take to move from peer to supervisor, and what worked best? What advice would you give to a new supervisor based on your experience making this important transition?
4. What are the four components of successful delegation? Based on your experience as a delegator, which parts, if any, do you find more difficult to carry out than the others? What makes them harder for you?
5. Page 11 of the book chapter describes the value of building relationships both inside and outside the organization to produce better outcomes. What strategies can you use to broaden your reach and build strong, productive relationships?
6. How and why does a supervisor function as a "broker?"
7. What are the three most important ideas you gained from reading this chapter that you believe will help you become a better supervisor?

Learning activities

Activity 1.1 Learning from your best supervisor

If you are a new supervisor, think about your experience as an employee and your relationship to previous supervisors. Identify one supervisor with whom you had a productive relationship and identify the specific things that supervisor did to help you be successful on the job. Try to develop a comprehensive list of actions, skills, and behaviors that your supervisor did on a regular basis that had a direct impact on your work experience. Then select the specific skills or behaviors that you believe will be most valuable to you in your transition from employee to supervisor.

Activity 1.2 Assessing your supervisory skills

This activity is designed to help you reflect on what you hope to get out of this course based on an assessment of your current supervisory skills. Use these questions to carry out the assessment:

1. What do you consider your leadership and management strengths?
2. What areas of leadership and management capacity do you think need further development?
3. How do your unit's mission, vision, and values connect to the organization's mission, vision, and values?
4. How well do the members of your team understand the organization's goals, the unit's goals, and their individual goals?
5. What do you do regularly to support your team?
6. Do you ever include other teams in decision-making processes? How?
7. What is the biggest challenge you face right now as a supervisor?

Activity 1.3 Assessing your delegation quotient

To assess your understanding of and commitment to delegation as a supervisory skill, indicate whether you agree (A) or disagree (D) with each of the following statements by putting an A or D in the space preceding each statement.

____ 1. Delegation multiplies results through the division of duties.

____ 2. A supervisor should not delegate authority.

____ 3. A supervisor should not hold an employee responsible for the outcome of tasks that have not been delegated.

____ 4. It takes more time and effort to delegate and explain jobs than it does to do them yourself.

____ 5. Ultimate accountability for mistakes made by employees rests with the supervisor.

____ 6. Delegating routine duties to employees makes your team, your supervisor, and others think you are lazy.

____ 7. You should delegate jobs that you don't want to do yourself.

____ 8. Delegation should be used to develop employee skills.

____ 9. It is your job to get work done through the people on your team.

____ 10. You should take into account the likes and dislikes of the employee when assigning work.

____ 11. It is better to take work home every night than to burden your employees with your work.

____ 12. You should never overrule or reverse decisions made by employees who are working on a task you have delegated.

____ 13. It is your responsibility to explain the priority of a delegated task and to set a deadline for its completion.

____ 14. You should check in daily on the work you delegated.

____ 15. Delegation can be an effective motivational technique.

____ 16. A supervisor can challenge employees by delegating more work than they can handle.

____ 17. Longer projects or important assignments should be delegated in smaller chunks.

The most difficult thing about delegating work is [complete the *thought*]:

The tasks that I have the most difficulty delegating are [complete the *thought*]:

After you indicate whether you agree or disagree with each statement and complete the two statements about delegation difficulty, compare notes with other supervisors in your class to reach agreement on *agrees* and *disagrees,* and discuss what these statements tell you about how you approach delegation. If you are not working in a class, meet with one experienced supervisor or your own direct supervisor to review the statements and get further input on how to become a better delegator.

Activity 1.4 Becoming a successful supervisor

The graphic on page 13 of the book chapter identifies six characteristics of a successful supervisor:

1. Communication skills
2. Loyalty
3. Positive attitude
4. Desire for the job
5. Ability to delegate
6. Fairness.

Think about your supervisory experience, performance, and confidence, and then rate your current skill level on each of the characteristic using this three-point scale: (1) weak, (2) average, and (3) strong. If you feel comfortable seeking feedback from colleagues or employees, ask them to identify which of the five characteristics is your greatest strength and which is the area you need to work on the most, and then compare your assessment with that of others. Finally, select the characteristic that seems the most important to you at this point in your supervisory development and identify specific ways you will further enhance your skill in that area.

Activity 1.5 Doing supervision

One of the biggest challenges new and even veteran supervisors face is figuring out what successful supervisors do on a daily basis—meet, discuss, plan, organize, coach, give feedback, carry out specific technical tasks? The lessons that follow will provide more information on actions and outcomes that will help you define your role as a supervisor more clearly. This activity is designed to help make the supervisory process and role more concrete and tangible in the context of your organization. Follow these steps:

1. List five activities or functions that you think describe what a typical supervisor does or that define what you do on a regular basis as a supervisor. Be as specific as possible.

2. Talk with three experienced supervisors or managers in your department or organization and ask them to list the five most important activities or functions they do regularly as supervisors. Try to get spontaneous answers rather than giving them time to go home and think about your question.
3. Summarize all the activities or functions of supervisors from your list, the information from others, and the reading. Do you have twenty or more activities with lots of variety, or did you find many recurring activities from all sources?
4. What conclusions can you reach about your supervisory role based on this activity?

Be sure to keep your composite list in your lesson notebook so that you can revise and update it as needed in the lessons that follow.

Activity 1.6 Setting learning objectives

This activity is designed to help you set personal learning objectives for your participation in the course. Begin by reviewing the overall course objectives on page vi of this study guide. Then think about and respond to the following questions:

1. Why are you taking this course?
2. How do you feel about the course after finishing the first reading assignment and lesson? Are you more or less motivated? Why?
3. What is the best thing that could happen to you as a supervisor as a result of completing this course?
4. What specific steps will you take to stay motivated during the course and make sure you get the most out of this learning opportunity?
5. How do you hope to use what you learn from this course in your job?
6. What specific questions would you like to be able to answer about your job as a supervisor when you finish the course? Try to identify at least three questions that are on your mind at the outset.

After responding to the questions, list five learning objectives that complete this sentence:

When I finish this course, I hope to be able to...

1. ____________________
2. ____________________
3. ____________________
4. ____________________
5. ____________________

Once you complete your learning objectives worksheet, keep it with your course materials and review it after each lesson to check your progress and ensure that your objectives are still relevant.

TAKING IT FORWARD

Review the checklist on page 15 of Chapter 1 in *Effective Supervisory Practices* and the activities you have completed for this lesson. Select one skill or behavior you intend to pursue on the job to improve your supervisory success. Then, identify *three actions* you will take immediately to begin to carry out the skill or behavior. For example, you might decide to focus on improving your skill in delegating work to employees. Three actions you might take are to

1. Identify one or two specific activities that you are currently doing that you believe could be delegated to members of your team and decide who are the right people on your team to handle those tasks.
2. Meet with each employee to explain the task, the deadline, and your expectations.
3. Monitor progress on the task based on what you learned about successful supervision.

After you have tried the new skills on the job for at least one month, document what happened and what you have learned that can help you be more successful as you continue to carry out the new behaviors and skills.

Lesson 2:
SUPERVISORY LEADERSHIP

Lesson objective:
To provide new ideas and practical advice on how to become a more successful leader.

Reading assignment:
Effective Supervisory Practices Fifth Edition, Chapter 2: Supervisory Leadership

Lesson outcomes:
When you finish this lesson, you should

- Be familiar with current thinking about leadership, and why it matters to you as a supervisor
- Know the primary sources of influence in your supervisory job and how they affect your leadership success
- Have a broader view of practices that will improve your leadership capacity
- Know what steps you can take to become a stronger supervisory leader.

Lesson overview

This lesson focuses on increasing your understanding of leadership theories and practices and beginning to develop your skills as a supervisory leader. The chapter emphasizes that behavior is a better predictor of effective leadership than specific traits and that a commitment to training and professional development during your supervisory career can increase your success as an effective leader. Major areas covered in the chapter that are important to your development as a successful supervisory leader are sources of influence, predictors of leadership success, leadership practices, the value of feedback for self-awareness, and leadership fitness.

Review questions

1. The book chapter begins with the following quote from President John Quincy Adams: "If your actions inspire others to dream more, learn more, do more, and become more, you are a leader." Think about someone who has inspired you to dream more, learn more, do more, and become more. Your source of inspiration can be someone who had a direct impact on your life, such as a parent or teacher, or someone who inspired you from a distance, such as a political leader, an author, or a historic figure. What specifically did that person do that inspired you?

2. Based on a careful review of the section in *Effective Supervisory Practices* that begins on page 18, entitled "What is leadership?" and drawing on your own knowledge and experience, write a definition of leadership.
3. What are the three primary sources of influence, and how do they affect your success as a supervisor?
4. What is the difference between leadership traits and leadership behaviors? Identify several examples of each to highlight the difference.
5. Identify and describe specific leadership practices covered in the chapter that you believe will enhance your skills as a successful leader.
6. What are the primary dimensions of leadership self-care?
7. What is emotional intelligence or EQ, and how does it contribute to leadership success?
8. What are the three most important ideas you gained from reading this chapter that you believe will help you become a better supervisor?

Learning activities

Activity 2.1 Leaders and leadership

Identify five people who you consider to be effective leaders. Then list three to five characteristics or skills that make each of them good leaders.

1. ____________________
2. ____________________
3. ____________________
4. ____________________
5. ____________________

What does your list of leaders and leadership skills tell you about your own approach to leadership? Which leader do you most want to be like, and what actions do you need to take to become a more effective leader?

Activity 2.2 Examining your leadership success

Describe two or three incidents in which you feel your leadership had an impact on specific outcomes or results in your department. What do these incidents have in common? What made you an effective leader in these situations? Ask others who were involved in those incidents to tell you what they thought made you an effective leader in these situations.

Activity 2.3 Seeking feedback for self-awareness

Being aware of your leadership strengths and areas that need further development can enhance your leadership effectiveness. One way to increase self-awareness is to gather information from others about their perceptions of your leadership style. To help you assess your progress in developing leadership skills and behavior, identify two individuals in your department who you know well, trust, and are in a position to observe or experience you as a supervisory leader. Explain to them what you are trying to accomplish through this course and what specific leadership areas you are focusing on. Then invite them to be resources over a specific timeframe during this course. Meet with your selected resources twice a month to get feedback on your leadership behaviors and any changes that they note. Keep notes on their feedback along with your other course materials.

TAKING IT FORWARD

Review the checklist on page 29 of Chapter 2 in *Effective Supervisory Practices* and the activities you have completed for this lesson. Select one skill or behavior you intend to take forward to focus on developing your leadership capacity. Then, identify three actions you will take immediately to begin to carry out the skill or behavior on the job and improve your leadership performance. After you have tried the new behaviors and skills for at least one month, document what happened and what you have learned that can help you be more successful as you continue to carry out the new behaviors and skills.

Lesson 3:
ETHICS

Lesson objective:
To ensure attention to ethics as a fundamental supervisory responsibility.

Reading assignment:
Effective Supervisory Practices Fifth Edition, Chapter 3: Ethics

Lesson outcomes:
When you finish this lesson, you should

- Know what ethics is, and why it is important to your role as a local government supervisor
- Be familiar with your organization's approach to ethics, including any ethics policy or code of conduct
- Understand the importance of modeling and coaching employees to ethical behavior
- Be aware of the ICMA Code of Ethics as a guiding resource for public sector ethics.

Lesson overview

This lesson is designed to deepen your understanding of ethics and provide tools to support ethical behavior and performance. It builds on the framework in Chapter 3 of the book and offers strategies for helping you grow as an ethical supervisor. A key message of the book chapter and this lesson is that, as a supervisor, you have dual ethical responsibilities: first, to manage your own ethical behavior and decision making, and then to be a model, coach, and resource to your employees to ensure that they share that commitment to ethics.

Review questions

1. Why does ethical behavior matter so much in public service?
2. Who is responsible for ethical behavior in an organization?
3. What are your primary roles as a supervisor related to ethics?
4. What are the three "*A*"s that help define ethics in action, and how do each of those guiding principles apply to your job?

5. What specific steps can you take in your work unit to (a) *model* ethical behavior, (b) *coach* employees on all aspects of their behavior, including ethics, and (c) *lead* employees to ethical behavior?
6. Page 32 in *Effective Supervisory Practices* makes this statement: "When one government employee behaves in an unethical way, it reflects on every government employee." Do you think this same statement can be made about employees in the private sector? Why or why not? Can you think of a situation when the actions of a government employee either in your organization or somewhere else reflected badly on you? How did that make you feel? What can you do as a supervisor to contribute to positive perceptions of government employees?
7. What are the six questions ICMA recommends for assessing whether a possible action is ethical? If your answer to the first question is *no*, what should you do next?
8. What are the three most important ideas you gained from reading this chapter that you believe will help you become a better supervisor?

Learning activities

Activity 3.1 What is ethics?

Write a memo to your staff explaining what ethics is, why it is so important in the public sector, and what your expectations are of your staff in relation to ethical behavior and ethical action. In preparing your memo, draw on the concepts and guidance in Chapter 3 of *Effective Supervisory Practices*, your own perspective on ethics, and resources in your government that support ethical behavior and action. After writing the memo and discussing it with others in your class, decide whether you want to share it with your staff and what you would hope to accomplish by providing the memo. Are there any risks or downsides of sending a memo to your staff about ethics? If not a memo, what strategies would you use to increase awareness of the importance of ethical behavior and ethical action?

Activity 3.2 Ethics in your organization

Most local governments have an ethics policy or code of conduct that describes behavior that is expected of all employees. Some governments have a designated ethics advisor or counselor to help employees deal with ethical challenges. Your success as an ethical supervisor begins with understanding your local government's approach to ethics. This activity is designed to connect you to your organization's ethical structure by carefully reviewing the code of ethics or values statement and analyzing how it applies to your day-to-day work. If you haven't previously reviewed the code of ethics, prepare a list of actions you will take on a regular basis to ensure that your organization's approach to ethics becomes an integral part of how you behave and what you expect of your employees.

Activity 3.3 Personal and professional values

Values are ideas, principles, or beliefs that really matter to you and that form the basis for ethical action. They reflect your sense of right and wrong and of what "ought to be." Make a list of the five most important *values that guide your personal life*. Then make a list of the five most important *values that guide your professional life*. Are your personal and professional values the same? If there are differences, what accounts for those differences? Lastly, make a list of five public service values that you think could be used to guide all local government managers, supervisors, and employees in decision making and daily actions. If there are differences among your personal, professional, and public service values lists, what accounts for those differences?

Activity 3.4 Making ethical decisions

Read the three supervisory situations on pages 45 to 47 of Chapter 3 in *Effective Supervisory Practices.* Think about the information in the situation, your experience as a supervisor, and what you are learning about ethics in this lesson. Then answer the four questions for each supervisory situation focusing particularly on what is the right thing to do. If you are facing a tough decision right now that has ethical implications, write down the details of the situation, and use the guide to ethical decision making on page 39 of the book chapter or the ethical decision tree on page 40 to help you decide what is the right thing to do in your own supervisory situation.

TAKING IT FORWARD

Review the checklist on page 44 of Chapter 3 in *Effective Supervisory Practices* and the activities you have completed for this lesson. Select *one* area related to ethics that you intend to take forward to improve your supervisory success, focusing both on your behavior as a supervisor and on your role as an ethical leader, model, and coach. For example, you might decide that you want to focus specifically on what you can do to regularly *model* ethical behavior in your work unit or to *coach* employees to increase their awareness of and attention to ethics in their daily work and lives. Then, identify *three actions* you will immediately take to begin to carry out the skill or behavior on the job and improve your performance as an ethical supervisor. After you have tried the actions on the job for at least one month, document what happened and what you have learned that can help you become an even more successful supervisor.

Unit II:

GETTING THE WORK DONE

2

This unit focuses on the **work** for which you and your team are responsible. It provides approaches to defining broad work goals, organizing to achieve agreed-upon goals, and connecting the work of your unit to the local government. The lessons also provide strategies, tools, and resources to ensure that your work unit produces desired results on time and within the budget.

Lesson 4: Strategic Planning, Management, and Evaluation

Lesson 5: Organizing Your Work and Time

Lesson 6: Working with the Budget

Lesson 4:
STRATEGIC PLANNING, MANAGEMENT, AND EVALUATION

Lesson objective:
To introduce strategic planning and operations planning as essential skills for getting the right things done well.

Reading assignment:
Effective Supervisory Practices Fifth Edition, Chapter 4: Strategic Planning, Management, and Evaluation

Lesson outcomes:
When you finish this lesson, you should

- Be familiar with your organization's vision and strategic plan
- Understand the important role planning plays in your supervisory effectiveness
- Know how to set goals and objectives for your work unit
- Understand the plan-do-check-act cycle as a tool for improving both work unit and individual employee performance
- Be able to distinguish between strategic questions and operational questions to monitor progress and results.

Lesson overview

Moving from being an individual doer to someone who is responsible for planning, managing, and evaluating the work of multiple people is a big transition for many supervisors. It requires a new set of skills that focus on achieving broad results and balancing immediate work responsibilities with a longer view of desired outcomes. This lesson focuses on those new skills and provides tools that will help you develop effective goals, plan work carefully, monitor progress, make needed adjustments, and provide regular feedback to employees to ensure that you achieve agreed-upon work unit goals.

Review questions

1. As a supervisor, what are your primary *planning* responsibilities?
2. What are the characteristics of successful strategic goals?

3. How does a procedures manual contribute to successful goal setting, planning, and managing work performance? What are the most important components of a good procedures manual?
4. Describe how the *plan-do-check-act cycle* contributes to overall work unit effectiveness.
5. Describe how to use the *plan-do-check-act cycle* to manage individual employee performance.
6. What is the difference between strategic planning and operational planning, and how do the two types of planning work together?
7. What are the major components of an operational plan?
8. What is continuous improvement, and why is it important to your role as a supervisor?
9. Chapter 4 concludes with this sentence: "Success for a supervisor is not getting everything done, but getting the *right* things done well." How do you know what the *right* things are, and how do you ensure that they are done *well*?
10. What are the three most important ideas you gained from reading this chapter that you believe will help you become a better supervisor?

Learning activities

Activity 4.1 Connecting your work unit to the organizational strategic plan

Many local governments have formally adopted strategic plans that define mission, values, and goals to guide the organization for several years. Your challenge as a supervisor is to support the organization's vision, mission, and goals through measureable goals and outcomes for your work unit. Begin by reviewing your organization's strategic vision and plans carefully and then complete these steps:

1. Identify up to *five specific ways* that you believe your unit supports the organization's vision and goals.
2. Using the guidelines and models for successful strategic goals on pages 52 to 53 of Chapter 4 in *Effective Supervisory Practices*, develop *five strategic goals* for your work unit to ensure that you are focusing on the right activities to reach the organization's desired vision.

3. After you have become familiar with the organization's strategic plan and practiced your skills at creating strategic goals, meet with your team to (a) discuss the organization's strategic plan; (b) ask the team to identify *five ways* the work unit supports the strategic plan's vision and goals; and (c) work together to develop strategic goals to guide your unit's work over the coming year.

Activity 4.2: From doer to planner

Effective supervisors spend a significant amount of time planning to ensure that the unit is getting the right things done. But the transition from *doer* of tasks to *planner* of work to be done by others can be difficult. This activity is designed to help you become more comfortable with and aware of your planning role by monitoring how much time you spend planning in a typical work week. Begin by creating a log in your paper or electronic notebook where you can keep track of all of your activities over at least a five-day period, following these guidelines:

1. Record each major activity as your day progresses including the starting and ending time for each activity.
2. Each time your attention shifts to a new area, record the new activity.
3. At the end of five days, put a P next to every activity that you would classify as *planning* based on the information in the chapter. Then further classify these planning activities as *strategic planning* (SP) or *operational planning* (OP).
4. Calculate the approximate amount of time spent on planning based on the starting and stopping times in your log.
5. Finally, assess whether you spent a significant amount of time planning to ensure that the unit is getting the right things done. Did you spend more time on planning than other functions? If not, what types of activities consumed large segments of your time, for example, doing technical work yourself, monitoring progress on assigned tasks, and coaching or training employees to help them get their work done?

A time or activity log is a useful tool for assessing whether you are focusing on getting the right things done and, if not, what activities and tasks are consuming time that might be better spent on critical planning and managing responsibilities. The log can also help you assess how effectively you are paying attention to the entire *plan-do-check-act cycle* by recording all activities over several weeks and categorizing them as P, D, C, or A.

Activity 4.3 Planning for the unexpected

Even with the best planning, unexpected events occur which may require major shifts and adjustments in work plans and schedules. So successful supervisors try to plan for the unexpected by thinking in advance about what could happen that would affect the work unit, preparing contingency plans, and building some time into regular schedules to deal with the unexpected. Think about an unexpected situation that could have a major impact on your team's ability to carry out scheduled work and meet deadlines, such as (a) half of the team comes down with the flu, leaving you short-staffed for routine service delivery or a major project that is due within the next week; (b) a piece of equipment that is essential to day-to-day operations breaks down, and replacement/repairs will take more than a week; or (c) your supervisor gives your team a major new project to complete in five days for the city manager while sustaining daily operations. Or, you can think about a specific issue that has occurred in your unit and that is a source of concern. Then consider these questions:

1. What specific steps would you take to deal with the emergency and stay on top of the regular work load?
2. How would you decide what already planned activities could be delayed if you conclude that everything can't get done?
3. What would you tell your supervisor about the impact of this unexpected emergency and how you plan to handle it?
4. What would you do if it becomes clear that you can't do both, that is, you can't respond to the unexpected situation and also meet agreed upon service requirements or deadlines?

Activity 4.4 Developing a vision statement

Read the two supervisory situations on page 65 of Chapter 4 in *Effective Supervisory Practices*. Think about the information in each situation, your experience as a supervisor, and what you have learned in this lesson. Then answer the three questions for each of the supervisory situations including creating a vision statement. Or, use the same three questions for your work unit, including crafting a vision statement for your team, writing three goals that will contribute to the city's vision, and deciding how to involve your employees in the vision-writing and goal-setting processes.

TAKING IT FORWARD

Review the checklist on page 64 of Chapter 4 in *Effective Supervisory Practices* and the review questions and activities you have worked on for this lesson. Select *one* skill or behavior you intend to take forward to improve your supervisory success in getting the right things done well through effective planning, managing, and evaluating your work unit's performance. Then, identify *three actions* you will take immediately to begin to carry out the skill or behavior on the job and improve your supervisory performance. After you have tried the new behaviors and skills on the job for at least one month, document what happened and what you have learned that can help you be more successful as you continue to carry out the new behaviors and skills.

Lesson 5:
ORGANIZING YOUR WORK AND TIME

Lesson objective:
To provide tools and resources for becoming a well-organized supervisor.

Reading assignment:
Effective Supervisory Practices Fifth Edition, Chapter 5: Organizing Work and Time

Lesson outcomes:
When you finish this lesson, you should

- Understand the importance of planning to help you manage multiple responsibilities
- Be better equipped to set priorities and manage assignments, paperwork, and e-mail
- Have some new ideas about how to conquer procrastination
- Know how to get the most out of meetings.

Lesson overview

Successfully managing your supervisory workload and that of your employees requires increased attention to planning and use of tools to help you organize work and time. This lesson introduces you to practical methods for becoming better organized, making informed choices about how you spend your time, and avoiding such pitfalls as procrastination and interruptions.

Review questions

1. What is the difference between "importance" and "urgency" in your work tasks? Identify some examples of important tasks that you've worked on recently and some urgent ones.
2. Describe the four boxes in the "Eisenhower Matrix" and how they can help you manage your workload.
3. What factors should you consider when prioritizing tasks? How do you know what are your highest priority tasks versus tasks that can wait for your attention?
4. How can you maximize the value of e-mail for quick communication without letting it become a time waster? According to the chapter, studies show that if you check an e-mail upon receiving an alert, you

will consume more than twenty-three minutes before getting back to what you were working on before the interruption. If you are a frequent e-mail user, test that finding for one week to determine whether e-mail is a time waster for you. Then decide specific steps you can take to minimize this time waster.

5. Identify three causes of procrastination that you have confronted and specific actions you can take to overcome those causes.
6. What are the four basic types of meetings and the primary purpose of each? Which type of meeting do you use most regularly?
7. What is the best way to maximize meeting time? What specific steps have you found most useful for maximizing the success of your meetings?
8. What are the three most important ideas you gained from reading this chapter that you believe will help you become a better supervisor?

Learning activities

Activity 5.1 Prioritizing and scheduling your work

Setting priorities will help ensure that you and your employees focus on the most important tasks rather than responding primarily to the urgent. Using the *ABC-123* method on pages 69 to 71 of Chapter 5, develop a to-do list at the beginning of a week for work activities that require your time and attention. Then, follow these steps to prioritize and schedule your work for the week:

1. Write an A next to every high-priority item, a C next to every low-priority item, and a B next to every item that deserves medium priority.
2. Review the A items and put a 1 next to the tasks you must complete first, a 2 next to the second highest priority A items, and so on.
3. Mark the highest-priority B item with a 1, the next highest B with a 2, and so on.
4. Move your tasks to your calendar to schedule the time you need to complete each one during the coming week.

Use your prioritized, scheduled plan to guide your work for the week. At the end of the week, assess your success prioritizing and scheduling tasks using these questions:

1. Did you complete all of the tasks for the week? If not, what interfered with your success—the addition of unexpected tasks, urgent items that bumped important ones, too many items on the list for the available time, what else?
2. Of the tasks you did complete, were they mostly A priorities? Did any C items make it to your schedule and take up time? Did you find it difficult to distinguish A from C priorities?
3. In general, did the exercise of setting priorities and scheduling time help you be more productive? What can you do going forward to become more skilled at setting priorities and scheduling time based on those priorities?

Activity 5.2 Managing time wasters

Time wasters—activities that are neither important nor urgent—often consume a lot of available work time. Becoming more aware of recurring activities that waste valuable time is an important step toward minimizing their impact. To increase your awareness of the impact of time wasters, for two days keep a log of activities that you would classify as not important and not urgent (initiated by you and others) and estimate the amount of time these "wasters" consumed. After two days, review your log to assess whether the items you listed were indeed time wasters and what you can do to make better use of your time in the future. There may be some items on your list that feel like time wasters that might have been important to someone else, so be sure to assess each item carefully.

Activity 5.3 Assessing your delegation progress

Effective delegation is an essential supervisory skill to help you accomplish your unit goals, develop employee competence, and manage your work load. In Lesson 1, Activity 1.3, you were asked to assess your delegation quotient as you began this course. Review your responses on the worksheet and the section of this chapter on the "*do it, delegate it, defer it, delete it*" strategy for managing work. Then, reassess your delegation quotient and identify specific steps you can take, effective immediately, to become a more confident and successful delegator.

Activity 5.4 Overcoming procrastination

Review the causes of procrastination on page 77 of Chapter 5 in *Effective Supervisory Practices*. Then select the one cause that you encounter most often and that relates to a task or responsibility you are currently facing. Develop a plan for overcoming your tendency to procrastinate using the tips in the chapter and your own experience. The next time you find yourself procrastinating on something important, implement your work plan immediately to eliminate or minimize obstacles to making progress on your responsibilities.

Activity 5.5 Planning and managing a great meeting

Review the section on pages 76 to 80 of *Effective Supervisory Practices* on managing meetings, including the four basic types of meetings and the six steps for planning and leading better meetings. Then plan and carry out a great meeting with your team following these steps:

4. Decide what type of meeting you are scheduling by clarifying its primary purpose.
5. Prepare an agenda to further clarify the purpose of the meeting, the specific items you will cover, the time required for the meeting to accomplish the purpose, the required participants, and the people who will make presentations or lead discussions.
6. Contact the people who will make presentations or lead discussions and provide enough information to help them prepare for their role at the meeting.
7. Distribute the agenda at least one day in advance of the meeting to all participants; include any guidance to participants on how they should prepare for the meeting
8. Lead the meeting following the general guidelines on pages 78 to 80 of *Effective Supervisory Practices* and your own experience as a meeting leader. Be sure to encourage active participation by all attendees and listen carefully to their comments and input.
9. Summarize key points, follow-up action items, and responsibilities at the end of the meeting and set the time for the next meeting if required.
10. Send out a follow-up e-mail confirming the meeting outcomes and the next meeting date.

After the meeting, take some time to assess its effectiveness. Did you accomplish your outcomes? Was the time productive? Did team members participate actively? What can you do at the next meeting to make it even more productive? To further assess the effectiveness of your meeting, check with one or two participants to get their feedback on the value and success of the meeting.

Activity 5.6 Practicing getting organized

Read the two supervisory situations on pages 80 to 81 of Chapter 5 in *Effective Supervisory Practices*. Think about the information in each situation, your experience as a supervisor, and what you have learned in this lesson. Then answer the questions for the supervisory situations taking into account both the specifics of the situations and how they might apply to your local government.

TAKING IT FORWARD

Review the checklist on page 80 of Chapter 5 in *Effective Supervisory Practices* and the review questions and activities you have worked on for this lesson. Select *one* skill, behavior, or concept related to organizing your time and work that you intend to take forward to improve your supervisory success. Then, identify *three actions* you will take immediately to begin to carry out the skill or behavior on the job or apply the concept to improve your supervisory performance. After you have worked on these actions for at least one month, document what happened and what you have learned that can help you become a better organized and more productive supervisor.

Lesson 6:
WORKING WITH THE BUDGET

Lesson objective:
To enhance understanding of the importance of the local government budget as a supervisory tool and resource.

Reading assignment:
Effective Supervisory Practices Fifth Edition, Chapter 6: Working with the Budget

Lesson outcomes:
When you finish this chapter, you should

- Know about the importance of the local government budget in general and why it matters to you as a supervisor
- Understand your roles and responsibilities in the budget process
- Be familiar with your local government's approach to budgeting and the language, terms, and components that tell the budget story
- Know how you can have an impact on the overall direction of the budget to support division and program work goals
- Be more comfortable with developing and working with the budget.

Lesson overview

The local government budget is a powerful resource and tool. It translates policies into action, tells the public what services they can expect and how their tax dollars will be spent, defines how the organization will carry out its overall goals and program priorities for a specified period, and gives you the authority to get your job done on a daily basis. This lesson is designed to increase your knowledge of and comfort with local government budgeting and its connection to your supervisory roles and responsibilities.

Review questions

1. What are the three primary functions of the local government budget? How do each of those functions relate to your job as a supervisor?

2. What is a fiscal year and how does it affect your work? What are the start and end dates for your local government's fiscal year?
3. Most local governments have two separate budgets: the operating budget and the capital budget. What is the primary purpose of each budget, and how do they differ?
4. The chapter provides three examples of formats for the operating budget. What are the three formats? What budget format does your local government use?
5. What are the six steps in the budget process? What is the role of the supervisor in each step? Which steps, if any, have you already been involved in? Would you do anything differently on those steps based on what you are learning in this lesson?
6. What can you do to increase the likelihood that you will get the budget allocation needed to carry out your work goals?
7. What steps can you as a supervisor take to have an impact on your local government's financial success?
8. If you are a sports fan, why do you think Mayor Henry Maier called the budget process "the world series of municipal government?" Based on your knowledge of and experience with your local government's budget, do you agree with that observation? Why or why not?
9. What is performance measurement, and how does it relate to the annual budget? What are the five categories that are typically used for performance measures? If your local government uses performance measures in its annual budget, what categories does it use more often?
10. Does your local government use any other budgets in addition to the annual operating and capital budgets? If so, what are those other budgets and why are they separate from the two major budgets?
11. What are the three most important ideas you gained from reading this chapter that you believe will help you become a better supervisor?

Learning activities

Activity 6.1 Getting to know your local government budget

If you haven't previously done so, get a copy of your local government's operating and capital budgets and review them to get a sense of the format, key messages, and any information that seems relevant to your department, division, and unit. Review the sections of Chapter 6 in *Effective Supervisory Practices* that describe the functions of the budget (pages 85 to 87) and the different purposes of the budget document (page 92). Identify how your local government's budget document carries out those functions and purposes. What have you learned about working with the budget from this process? What do you need to do to increase your knowledge of and comfort with the budget process?

Activity 6.2 Preparing for a budget process

If you have not participated in a budget cycle for your local government as a supervisor, find out what the schedule is likely to be for the next budget cycle. Using the information in the chapter, start preparing now, including (a) learning what your role will be, (b) collecting the kind of information that you might be asked to provide, (c) outlining what you might ask for to meet your department's needs, and (d) generally increasing your comfort with what will be expected of you during the next cycle. If possible, talk to another supervisor in your department or division to learn more about the process and how you can best prepare for it. If you have participated in the budget process before starting this course, review what you requested, how it was received, what results you achieved, and what you might change or do better during the next budget cycle.

Activity 6.3 Practicing budget skills

Read the two supervisory situations on pages 100 to 101 of Chapter 6. Think about the information in each situation, your experience as a supervisor, and what you have learned in this lesson. Then answer the questions for the supervisory situations taking into account both the specifics of the situations and how they might apply to your local government.

TAKING IT FORWARD

Review the checklist on page 100 of *Effective Supervisory Practices* Chapter 6 and the review questions and activities you have worked on for this lesson. Select *one* skill, behavior, or concept related to working with the budget that you intend to take forward to improve your supervisory success. Then, identify *three actions* you will take immediately to begin to carry out the skill or behavior on the job or apply the concept to improve your supervisory performance. After you have worked on these actions for at least one month, document what happened and what you have learned that can help you be more successful as a supervisor when it comes to working with the budget.

3

Unit III:

DEVELOPING YOUR TEAM

This unit focuses on the people who report to you and carry out your unit's work on a daily basis. It addresses several essential human resources skills that provide the foundation for a high-performing team. The lessons provide information, tools, resources, and strategies for selecting, developing, and communicating with the people who make up your team.

Lesson 7:
TEAM BUILDING

Lesson objective:
To provide tools, resources, and ideas for building a high-performing team.

Reading assignment
Effective Supervisory Practices Fifth Edition, Chapter 7: Team Building

Lesson outcomes:
When you finish this lesson, you should

- Be familiar with the characteristics of teams, stages in becoming a team, and steps for building a team
- Understand the value of teamwork in the workplace
- See yourself as a team builder and team leader
- Know what it means to empower a team
- Be ready to focus on strengthening and sustaining your team's performance.

Lesson overview

Getting the work of your unit done through other people is your primary job as a supervisor. Transforming a group of individuals into a high-performing team takes your supervisory role one step farther. Teamwork is about improving work processes, the work culture, quality of service, and the results citizens get for their tax dollars. This lesson focuses on the broad dimensions of team work and your role in building a successful team that achieves its goals, meets deadlines, and is committed to shared outcomes.

Review questions

1. What are some specific advantages of using teams to accomplish the business of government, taking into account the information in the chapter and your experience as a team member and team leader?
2. What are the four stages a group goes through on its way to becoming a team? At what stage is your current group/team?
3. Think about the best team experience you have ever had. Using the questions on pages 105 to 106 in Chapter 7 of *Effective Supervisory Practices,* figure out what made that team experience so successful, and what you can apply to your current role as a team leader.

4. What is a "reactive" organizational environment versus a "proactive" team environment? Which approach would you say generally applies to your organizational and team environment?
5. As the leader of an organizational team, what are your primary roles in accountability and decision making?
6. What are the seven steps to building a team?
7. What does it mean to "empower" your employees and strengthen your team? What specific steps can you take to empower employees, drawing on both the chapter and your experience?
8. What are the three most important ideas you gained from reading this chapter that you believe will help you become a better supervisor?

Learning activities

Activity 7.1 Assessing individual team skills

Being a successful team leader starts with being a successful team player. Use the following team-building skills checklist to assess your teamwork skills by assigning a number to how you handle each dimension: 3 (always), 2 (sometimes), 1(rarely/never). You can use the checklist in a variety of settings to become more aware of your team skills, including after you participate in a team meeting with colleagues and supervisors, when you are leading a meeting with your team/employees, or as part of a supervisory class discussion. To enhance your learning, ask others in your group/team to complete the same checklist and compare notes on what you observed and experienced with each other's behavior.

1. Did I create a relaxed, collegial atmosphere that supported and encouraged collaboration?
2. Did I participate actively in the discussion?
3. Did I help keep the discussion on track?
4. Did I understand and accept the task or focus of the discussion and what the team was working on?
5. Did I listen to others?

6. Did I feel comfortable disagreeing with others?
7. Did I feel comfortable when others disagreed with me?
8. Did I seek consensus or help the group move toward a shared conclusion?
9. Did I use my knowledge and skills during the session to help the group get its work done and move forward?

After using the checklist in several settings, identify areas where you consistently rate yourself high (3) or low (1) to identify your individual team strengths and weaknesses. Then concentrate on enhancing your weaker skills in future meetings.

Activity 7.2 Identifying team leadership skills

In Lesson 2, you were asked to identify five people whom you consider effective leaders and identify characteristics or skills that make them good leaders. This activity asks you to think about people you have experienced as particularly effective *team leaders*. You might start by revisiting your notes from Lesson 2 on effective leaders and their leadership skills. Did you identify *team leadership* as a strong skill for any of those leaders? Then think about a positive team experience you have had in your life and the person who led that team. Using the questions on pages 105 to 106 of Chapter 7 in *Effective Supervisory Practices*, identify five specific skills that leader relied on to create a great team.

Activity 7.3 Assessing team effectiveness

Beginning on page 112, this chapter in *Effective Supervisory Practices* identifies seven steps to help you, as a supervisor, build a close-knit, highly motivated, and productive work team. The following checklist, which is based on the seven steps, provides a way to assess the overall effectiveness of your team and to identify areas for further work. Assign a number to each statement assessing how you and your team work together using the following scale: 3 (always), 2 (sometimes), 1(rarely/never). You can use the checklist individually, in a discussion with others in your class, or with members of your team to enhance overall effectiveness.

1. Team members know how they fit into the organizational system beyond their immediate boundaries.
2. The team meets regularly using established and understood ground rules.
3. Team members understand broad organizational goals/outcomes and how the work unit affects those outcomes.
4. Team members are comfortable offering solutions to problems and are confident that you want their input, feedback, and constructive criticism.
5. Team members know they can speak honestly, raise concerns, and share frustrations with you and other team members.
6. Team members have a say in setting standards for team performance.
7. Team members treat each other with respect, understand what your role is as the leader, and support and value different perspectives.

If you are using the assessment tool with your team, compare notes together to identify areas of agreement, obvious team strengths, and areas requiring improvement.

Activity 7.4 Practicing team-building skills

Read the two supervisory situations on pages 120 to 121 of Chapter 7 in *Effective Supervisory Practices*. Think about the information in each situation, your experience as a supervisor, and what you have learned in this lesson. Then answer the questions for each supervisory situation, taking into account both the specifics of the situations and how they might apply to your local government.

TAKING IT FORWARD

Review the checklist on page 119 of *Effective Supervisory Practices* and the review questions and activities you have worked on for this lesson. Select *one* area related to building your team that you want to focus on and identify *three actions* you will take immediately to begin to strengthen team performance. After you have worked on these actions for at least one month, document what happened and what you have learned that can help you be more successful as a supervisor when it comes to strengthening your team.

Lesson 8:
COMMUNICATING WITH EMPLOYEES

Lesson objective:
To provide a framework for and guidance on improving communication skills.

Reading assignment:
Effective Supervisory Practices Fifth Edition, Chapter 8: Communicating with Employees

What you should know:
When you finish this lesson, you should

- Understand the importance of communication for successful supervision
- Be familiar with the components of the communication process
- Be able to recognize and deal with barriers to effective communication
- Have some ideas about how electronic communication and social media fit into your communication repertoire
- Understand how diversity in the workplace creates communication challenges.

Lesson overview

Effective communication is an essential part of successful supervision, in part because you spend a large percentage of your time every day communicating in some form. This lesson focuses on tools, resources, and strategies for helping you to become a better communicator, which will help you become a better supervisor. The chapter provides valuable information on the communication process, nonverbal messages, barriers to effective communication, active listening, electronic communication and social media, and communicating with a diverse workforce.

Review questions

1. What are the six components of the communication process?
2. What is the difference between one-way and two-way communication? Which do you use more often in your day-to-day interaction with employees? Which is the more effective form of communication, and why is it more effective?

3. What are some examples of nonverbal communication? How does nonverbal communication affect whether you get your message across? Are you aware of your nonverbal cues when communicating? What can you do to increase your awareness of nonverbal cues?
4. Identify three barriers to communication that you experience regularly and ways you can overcome these barriers.
5. Page 131 of Chapter 8 in *Effective Supervisory Practices* contains this statement: "True listening goes beyond merely hearing: it means understanding what the other person is saying." What steps can you take as a supervisor to show that you truly understand what is being communicated? How does "active listening" differ from just listening to what someone is saying?
6. What steps can you take to provide feedback to an employee when you encounter resistance or resentment?
7. What are some advantages and risks of using electronic media to communicate with employees? Why is e-mail sometimes alienating? What steps can you take to facilitate appropriate use of e-mail?
8. Give some examples of language that might be interpreted as stereotyping. What steps should you keep in mind when working with a diverse group of employees?
9. What are the three most important ideas you gained from reading this chapter that you believe will help you become a better supervisor?

Learning Activities

Activity 8.1 Elements of good communication

Each of the following items is important for effective communication with employees. Review the list carefully and add any items that you think belong on the list. Then, identify the *three to five elements* that are most important to your specific job and to working with your employees. Put an asterisk (*) next to these elements, and note why they are so important to your success as a supervisor. Then, answer the three questions following the list.

1. Seeking clarification when you think an employee may not understand what you are saying.

2. Reading nonverbal messages and body language.
3. Considering who the receiver is and tailoring the message to him or her.
4. Recognizing the accomplishments of employees and praising good work.
5. Checking in with the work team regularly, even when there are no problems.
6. Balancing positive and negative feedback.
7. Giving feedback on performance promptly and regularly.
8. Soliciting feedback about your own performance or supervisory style.
9. Allowing employees to disagree with your opinions.
10. Listening to and addressing feelings as well as words.
11. Giving undivided attention to an employee who has come to you for help.
12. Waiting for an employee to finish talking without interrupting.
13. Other:
14. Other:
15. Other:

Which of these communication skills do you believe is your strongest?

Which of these communication skills do you believe is your weakest?

What steps can you take to improve communication weaknesses?

Activity 8.2 Examining nonverbal cues

Review the list of nonverbal cues illustrated on page 128 of Chapter 8 in *Effective Supervisory Practices*. Then, dedicate one day in your workplace to becoming more aware of your nonverbal cues, focusing particularly on using positive cues (open and interested) and minimizing negative cues (closed, angry, nervous, and bored). At the end of the day, record what you learned about your nonverbal cues and steps you can take to improve *how* you are communicating as well as *what* you are communicating.

Activity 8.3 Giving feedback

Effective supervisors give regular, unsolicited feedback to their employees. After reading this chapter, prepare a list of guidelines that will ensure that the feedback you provide is understood and received. Then, using the information on giving feedback on pages 133 to 135 of the *Effective Supervisory Practices* chapter, find at least one opportunity to provide positive feedback on performance. After you finish giving the positive feedback, jot down some notes about what went well, how the employee reacted, and how you can give positive feedback even more successfully the next time.

Activity 8.4 Practicing communication skills

Read the two supervisory situations on pages 140 to 143 of Chapter 8 in *Effective Supervisory Practices*. Think about the information in each situation, your experience as a supervisor, and what you have learned in this lesson. Then answer the questions for each supervisory situation, taking into account both the specifics of the situations and how they might apply to your local government.

TAKING IT FORWARD

Review the checklist on page 140 of *Effective Supervisory Practices* and the review questions and activities you have worked on for this lesson. Select *one* area related to improving your communication skills that you want to focus on and identify *three actions* you will take immediately to begin to become a better communicator. After you have worked on these actions for at least one month, document what happened and what you have learned that can help you be a more successful communicator.

Lesson 9:
SELECTING, ONBOARDING, AND DEVELOPING NEW EMPLOYEES

To explore supervisory roles in selecting, orienting, and developing employees.

Reading assignment:
Effective Supervisory Practices Fifth Edition, Chapter 9: Selecting, Onboarding, and Developing New Employees

Lesson outcomes:
When you finish this lesson, you should

- Be familiar with your organization's recruitment process and your role in it
- Understand what onboarding is, and how it contributes to team effectiveness
- Know how to create a successful employee development program.

Lesson overview

This lesson focuses on your role in selecting and developing employees, both to enhance their effectiveness and to help you get work done with and through other people. It covers your role in key human resources functions including selecting the right person for a position; welcoming, educating, and orienting new employees in your unit; and ensuring that your employees have the knowledge and skills to succeed on the job. These functions all require a close partnership between you and your organization's human resources department.

Review questions

1. What are the components of a complete and legally compliant job description?
2. What are the most important steps to follow in preparing for a successful interview with a candidate for a job in your unit?
3. What is behavioral interviewing? What are some examples of questions you might use to assess past behavior and how that behavior relates to the job you are filing?
4. What are some examples of questions that you should *not* ask in an interview because of legal requirements?

5. What are the primary components of an effective employee onboarding program?
6. What are the most important things a new employee in your unit needs to know to be successful in his or her job?
7. What specific questions should you take into account when planning how you will train and develop employees?
8. What is a job aid, and how does it help new employees succeed?
9. What are the five steps in a typical employee onboarding and development process?
10. What are the three most important ideas you gained from reading this chapter that you believe will help you become a better supervisor?

Learning activities

Activity 9.1 Writing an effective job description

To increase your understanding of and skill in creating complete and legally compliant job descriptions, get copies of the descriptions for all of the jobs in your work unit. Review each one and compare it to the key components identified on page 147 of Chapter 9 as important for a complete job description. What, if anything, would you add or change in the descriptions to make them even stronger? Then, identify a job that you might want to add to your unit at some point, and write a complete and legally compliant job description for that position.

Activity 9.2 Conducting a successful interview

Consider this situation: you have been asked to be on a panel to interview candidates for another supervisory position in your department. Select a supervisory position with which you are fairly familiar and review the steps on pages 147 to 148 of Chapter 9 in *Effective Supervisory Practices* that outline how to prepare for a successful interview and the sample interview questions on page 150. Then, prepare a list of questions you would want to ask a person applying for a supervisory position in your department and identify the materials you would need to conduct the interview.

Activity 9.3 Engaging new employees

Pages 155 to 156 of Chapter 9 provides nine steps for helping new employees get off to a good start. Using that information as a starting point, develop a list of steps for engaging new employees that is specific to your work unit, including highlighting the information and resources you think are essential to employee success.

Activity 9.4 The employee onboarding and development process

Review the graphic on page 155 of Chapter 9, which identifies five steps in an employee onboarding and development process. Think about what you have learned in this lesson and processes that are in place in your organization. Then assess your overall effectiveness in each of the steps, including whether you have carried out steps in engaging any new employees; steps on which you think you have been particularly effective; and areas that require more work or focus.

Activity 9.5 Practicing interviewing and onboarding skills

Read the two supervisory situations on pages 161 to 163 of Chapter 9. Think about the information in each situation, your experience as a supervisor, and what you have learned in this lesson. Then answer the questions for the supervisory situations taking into account both the specifics of the situations and how they might apply to your local government.

TAKING IT FORWARD

Review the checklist on page 161 of *Effective Supervisory Practices* and the review questions and activities you have worked on for this lesson. Select *one* area related to selecting, onboarding, and developing new employees that you want to focus on and identify *three actions* you will take immediately to improve your effectiveness in selecting and developing employees. After you have worked on these actions for at least one month, document what happened and what you have learned that can help you be more successful as a supervisor when it comes to selecting and engaging new employees.

Unit IV:

ENSURING HIGH PERFORMANCE AND RESULTS

4

The lessons in this unit continue the focus on the **people** who work for you, emphasizing your role in ensuring high performance. Lessons cover essential supervisory roles related to accountability, performance evaluation, and motivation.

Lesson 10:
ACCOUNTABILITY IN THE WORKPLACE

Lesson objective:
To introduce the concept of accountability and why it is important to successful supervision.

Reading assignment:
Effective Supervisory Practices Fifth Edition, Chapter 10: Accountability in the Workplace

Lesson outcomes:
When you finish this lesson, you should

- Understand the continuum of accountability
- Know your role in ensuring that team members are accountable to you, each other, and the public
- Recognize the connection between accountability and feedback
- Be familiar with your organization's approach to performance improvement and disciplinary action
- Know how to carry out a successful disciplinary process that leads to improved performance.

Lesson overview

As a supervisor, you must ensure that employees do what they are expected to do for the public they serve and that there are consequences for failing to carry out those defined expectations. Accountability involves both negative and positive responses to performance. Letting employees know what they are doing well is just as important as drawing their attention to unacceptable performance. This lesson will help you understand what accountability is and what you as a supervisor can and should do to ensure that employees meet established expectations and do what they say they will do as a member of your work team.

Review questions

1. Based on your experience in an organization and the information in this *Effective Supervisory Practices* chapter, what is accountability? How do you hold your employees accountable to you, to each other, and to the public they serve? What does your supervisor do to hold you accountable?
2. What are the components of a continuum of accountability?

3. Provide some examples of how you can use praise, recognition, and rewards to encourage accountability and high performance. Which tool do you find most useful for giving positive feedback to your employees?
4. What is a performance improvement plan, and under what circumstances would you use one?
5. What is progressive discipline, and under what circumstances would you initiate progressive discipline?
6. Drawing on the information in the chapter and knowledge of your organization's disciplinary policies, identify examples of specific actions you might take as part of a progressive disciplinary process.
7. If you work in an organization that has collective bargaining, what different steps/actions should you keep in mind when initiating disciplinary action?
8. What are the three most important ideas you gained from reading this chapter that you believe will help you become a better supervisor?

Learning activities

Activity 10.1 Providing regular feedback

Ongoing communication is crucial to accountability. After reading this chapter and reviewing the information in Chapter 8 on communicating with employees, prepare a list of steps you will take regularly to provide feedback to your team to ensure accountability. Then, using the information on giving feedback and praise on pages 167 to 170 of Chapter 10, find at least one opportunity to provide positive feedback when you see a team member doing something right. After you finish giving the positive feedback, jot down some notes about what went well, how the employee reacted, and how you can give positive feedback even more successfully the next time.

Activity 10.2 Enhancing your coaching skills

Just like a coach on the playing field or an orchestra conductor, an effective team leader sets the standard, provides the tools, gives advice when it is needed, and lets the team play to the best of its ability. Using the eight principles to improve your coaching success (pages 170 to 171 of Chapter 10 in *Effective Supervisory Practices*), identify an opportunity for having a coaching discussion with an employee or practice these coaching skills with a colleague in your class in preparation for an actual discussion. Then reflect on choices you made about how to conduct the coaching session, steps with which you felt particularly comfortable or successful, and principles that seemed to cause the most difficulty or discomfort.

Activity 10.3 Selecting the best accountability option

Chapter 10 in *Effective Supervisory Practices* highlights several different tools for ensuring accountability and dealing with performance or personal employee challenges. Four major tools covered in the chapter are (1) coaching to improve work performance; (2) counseling to address personal challenges or needs; (3) performance improvement plans to provide a more rigorous and structured form of coaching, and (4) disciplinary action when other options fall short. Choosing the right approach for the presenting issue is an important step to produce the best results. For each of the following situations, choose which of the four tools you would use and explain why you think that approach would be most appropriate.

1. Stan has been about ten minutes late to work almost every day during the past month.
2. John has been on staff for about a month and already has made several costly mistakes.
3. Mary tells you she is unhappy with her job.
4. After three months on the job and several coaching sessions, John is continuing to make costly mistakes.
5. Laura tells you she is overwhelmed by her workload.
6. Jeremy has been seen drinking with colleagues at lunch.
7. Stan continues to arrive late to work several days a week despite several reminders about work hours.
8. Sara repeatedly ignores safety procedures.
9. Lavagna asks you for advice on disciplining her teenager.
10. Jim failed to complete an essential job on time even after being reminded several times about the deadline and its urgency.

Activity 10.4 Developing a performance improvement plan

When coaching does not raise employee performance to a desired level, a performance improvement plan may be a useful strategy. Consider this situation: Sara has repeatedly ignored safety procedures on the job despite several coaching sessions explaining the importance of paying attention to those procedures and the risks her lack of attention pose to herself and her colleagues. Using the five steps on pages 174 to 175 of Chapter 10, develop a plan and an overall approach to improving Sara's performance. Or, identify an opportunity in your work unit to develop a performance improvement plan with an employee who has not responded to coaching and feedback. Pay particular attention to the steps that cause you the most difficulty, anxiety, or discomfort.

Activity 10.5 Practicing accountability skills

Read the three supervisory situations on pages 184 to 186 of Chapter 10. Think about the information in each situation, your experience as a supervisor, and what you have learned in this lesson. Then answer the questions for the supervisory situations taking into account both the specifics of the situations and how they might apply to your local government.

TAKING IT FORWARD

Review the checklist on page 183 of *Effective Supervisory Practices* and the review questions and activities you have worked on for this lesson. Select *one* area related to accountability in the workplace that you want to focus on and identify *three actions* you will take immediately to improve your effectiveness in ensuring accountability. After you have worked on these actions for at least one month, document what happened and what you have learned that can help you be more successful as a supervisor when it comes to accountability in the workplace.

Lesson 11:
EVALUATING PERFORMANCE

Lesson objective:
To provide information, resources, and tools for carrying out positive and successful performance evaluations.

Reading assignment:
Effective Supervisory Practices Fifth Edition, Chapter 11: Evaluating Performance

Lesson outcomes:
When you finish this lesson, you should

- Have a positive approach, attitude, and commitment to performance evaluation
- Be familiar with your organization's approach to performance evaluation
- Understand your role in carrying out the evaluation cycle
- Know how to establish performance criteria
- Be better able to conduct a successful evaluation interview.

Lesson overview

This lesson focuses on ensuring a broad understanding of and positive commitment to performance evaluation as an essential management tool. It emphasizes the benefits of performance evaluation to clarify job expectations, address needed changes in the work environment, improve performance, acknowledge successful performance, hold low performers accountable for their shortcomings, and communicate and connect with team members.

Review questions

1. Based on your experience evaluating performance and being evaluated, what do you see as the three benefits of a well-designed and successfully conducted performance evaluation process?
2. Explain how performance evaluation is "a year-long process rather than an event."
3. How can you, as a supervisor, ensure that there are no surprises during a formal evaluation interview?

4. Identify *three myths* about performance evaluation that you have experienced or are aware of. Then identify *three realities* about performance evaluation that demonstrate its importance and impact.
5. What specific steps can you take to ensure that your employees understand the evaluation factors and goals against which their performance will be measured?
6. Chapter 11 in *Effective Supervisory Practices* states that a successful evaluation should focus on performance results, not on personality or personal shortcomings and failures. Give examples of performance results versus personality or personal shortcomings to demonstrate the difference between the two.
7. Identify the seven guidelines for conducting a successful evaluation interview.
8. What specific strategies will help you prepare for and carry out difficult evaluation interviews?
9. What are the characteristics of a legally acceptable performance evaluation system?
10. The chapter identifies five common performance evaluation errors. Select one of the errors that you have experienced or think poses a particular risk to many supervisors and identify ways you can avoid that error.
11. What are the three most important ideas you gained from reading this chapter that you believe will help you become a better supervisor?

Learning activities

Activity 11.1 Evaluating performance evaluations

To assess your attitude toward performance evaluations, indicate whether you agree (A) or disagree (D) with each of the following statements about both your work for this lesson and your experience by putting an A or D in the space preceding each statement.

____ 1. A performance evaluation is a waste of time, especially if it isn't tied to wages.

____ 2. One of the main reasons performance is evaluated is to motivate employees.

____ 3. Evaluations should only come at the end of a project or process.

____ 4. People don't like to have their performance reviewed by someone else.

____ 5. Performance evaluations are more important for new employees than for those with whom you have worked for a longer time.

____ 6. Employees should know how their supervisors feel about their performance before their annual evaluation meeting.

____ 7. The evaluation should be based on an employee's personality.

____ 8. Supervisors should not point out poor performance unless they can provide specific examples and suggestions for improvement.

____ 9. Most employees care about their work and what their supervisors think about their performance.

____ 10. A performance evaluation should include a comparison of different employees doing the same work.

____ 11. Employees should play a role in documenting and evaluating their own performance.

____ 12. Future performance goals should be set during the annual evaluation discussion.

After completing your assessment of each statement, compare notes with other supervisors in your class to reach agreement on *agrees* and *disagrees*. Then discuss what these statements tell you about your attitude toward performance appraisals. If you are not working in a class, meet with an experienced supervisor in your department or with your own direct supervisor to review the statements and discuss how you can maximize the benefits of the performance evaluation process for your employees.

Activity 11.2 Nurturing a positive view of performance evaluation

Your approach and attitude toward performance evaluation has a big impact on how your employees regard the process. In order to ensure that your team sees performance evaluation as a productive and beneficial experience, prepare an outline for leading a team discussion about the importance of the performance evaluation process to both individual and group success. Draw on the myths and realities table (page 191) and the opportunities and benefits discussion (page 192) of Chapter 11 as well as specific information about your organization's performance evaluation process to nurture a positive view among your team members. You can test your key messages with other supervisors in the class and, if appropriate, schedule a team meeting to discuss why the performance evaluation process is so important. The ideal time to have this discussion with your team is at the beginning of an evaluation cycle.

Activity 11.3 Embracing your organization's performance evaluation process and instrument

Your success in carrying out successful performance evaluations depends on understanding both the principles of performance evaluation as a management tool and the specifics of your organization's process and instrument. Whether you have used the process and instrument for a while or are new to it, spend time getting to know it in more depth, focusing particularly on

- The overall performance management schedule, including when you set goals with employees, when evaluations are scheduled (e.g., on the same date for all employees or on anniversary dates), and any interim reporting requirements.
- Evaluation factors that are used in the instrument, such as timeliness of work, customer service, and so on.
- The rating standard that you will use for the performance factors (e.g., excellent, good, poor).

If you have any questions about the performance evaluation process, discuss them with others in your supervisory class, with other supervisors in your department, or with your human resources director.

Activity 11.4 Handling difficult discussions

An evaluation discussion that will include negative feedback or with an employee who is dissatisfied, expecting negative feedback, or prone to confrontational conversation is difficult no matter how well prepared you are. If you have faced a difficult evaluation discussion in the past, review that conversation in light of the guidelines provided on page 198 of Chapter 11 in *Effective Supervisory Practices* and decide what you would do differently to ensure a more productive conversation. Or, think about an upcoming conversation that might be difficult and prepare a strategy for having a positive, productive discussion even if the content of the conversation may be negative.

Activity 11.5 Practicing performance evaluation skills

Read the three supervisory situations on pages 203 to 205 of Chapter 11. Think about the information in each situation, your experience as a supervisor, and what you have learned in this lesson. Then answer the questions for the supervisory situations taking into account both the specifics of the situations and how they might apply to your local government.

TAKING IT FORWARD

Review the checklist on page 203 of *Effective Supervisory Practices* and the review questions and activities you have worked on for this lesson. Select *one* area related to performance evaluations that you want to focus on and identify *three actions* you will take immediately to improve your effectiveness in using this essential management tool. After you have worked on these actions for at least one month, document what happened and what you have learned that can help you be more successful as a supervisor when it comes to creating a positive evaluation environment and evaluating your employees.

Lesson 12:
MOTIVATING EMPLOYEES

Lesson objective:
To enhance skills in energizing, inspiring, and motivating employees.

Reading assignment:
Effective Supervisory Practices Fifth Edition, Chapter 12: Motivating Employees

Lesson outcomes:
When you finish this lesson, you should

- Be familiar with theories of motivation that can guide your work as a supervisor
- Provide tools for tailoring motivational approaches to meet different employee needs and temperaments
- Be better equipped to motivate employees to carry out their responsibilities.

Lesson overview

Motivating employees is an essential and highly challenging supervisory role. It requires understanding of people and what makes them tick. This lesson focuses on *theories* of motivation, which are important in providing a framework for action and *strategies* for becoming a better motivator.

Review questions

1. What are the components of Abraham Maslow's hierarchy of needs? What needs on the ladder are most relevant to your role as a supervisor and your workplace?
2. According to Frederick Herzberg, what factors generally satisfy workers and what factors are likely to demotivate employees? Which of the motivators and demotivators can you, as a supervisor, influence the most?
3. What specific steps can you take to improve your relationships with your employees in order to minimize this potential source of dissatisfaction?
4. What are Daniel Pink's three motivational concepts? How do they each relate to and/or differ from Mazlow's and Herzberg's hierarchy of needs and motivational factors? Identify at least one step that you can take to motivate employees using Pink's three concepts.

5. What does the description of the Myers-Briggs Type Indicator temperaments on pages 215 to 220 of Chapter 12 tell you about your employees and how you can best motivate them? Which one of the four temperaments best describes you based on the information in the chapter?
6. How does the study of motivation affect your relationship with your manager? What steps can you take to "manage your manager?"
7. Some organizations are better than others at motivating employees. How would you rate your organization's motivational strategies? What are your organization's strengths in building motivation among employees and where could your organization improve?
8. How would you rate your overall motivation as a supervisor? After reviewing all the motivational theories, what motivates you the most?
9. What are the three most important ideas you gained from reading this chapter that you believe will help you become a better supervisor?

Learning activities

Activity 12.1 What does motivation mean to you?

To assess your understanding of and approach to motivation, indicate whether you agree (A) or disagree (D) with each of the following statements by putting an A or D in the space preceding each statement.

____ 1. You can motivate other people, particularly if they work for you.

____ 2. Some employees are unmotivated, and there is little you can do to change that.

____ 3. Food motivates a rat to run a maze.

____ 4. Employees who are motivated will remain so unless their jobs change.

____ 5. The best way to enhance motivation is to offer a salary increase or a bonus.

____ 6. You can identify motivated employees because they are the ones who work late and on weekends.

____ 7. Keeping employees challenged by letting them work independently on new assignments is the best way to keep them motivated.

____ 8. Publicity about the achievements of the local government, work team, and colleagues enhances motivation.

____ 9. Allowing others to participate in making decisions has a good effect on their work and will increase their motivation to contribute more.

____ 10. Most people want to do a good job.

After completing your assessment of each statement, compare notes with other supervisors in your class to reach agreement on *agrees* and *disagrees*. Then discuss what these statements tell you about steps you can take to motivate your employees drawing on the information in the chapter. If you are not working in a class, meet with an experienced supervisor in your department to review the statements about motivation, get another perspective on foundations of employee motivation, and increase your understanding of ways to motivate your employees.

Activity 12.2 Assessing the situation

Use the following questions to take a motivational temperature in your organization and to begin to think about how you can motivate your employees and yourself.

1. Generally, how motivated would you say members of your work team are?
2. Generally, how would you rate your own motivation?
3. What does your immediate supervisor do that motivates you?
4. What does your staff do that motivates you?
5. What do others do that frustrates or demotivates you?
6. What do you do that motivates your employees?
7. What do you do that may frustrate or demotivate your employees or colleagues?

Based on your assessment, develop a list of specific actions you can take now to help motivate your employees.

Activity 12.3 Creating your approach to motivation

Review all of the theories of motivation that are covered in Chapter 12 of *Effective Supervisory Practices* and think about your experience as both an employee and a supervisor. As part of your review, think about a supervisor who was particularly effective in motivating or inspiring you. What did he or she do to keep you motivated and inspired? Then, develop a framework for your own approach to energizing, inspiring, and motivating your employees.

Activity 12.4 Prioritizing motivational factors

Review the following list of factors that organizations have found can have a positive impact on employee motivation. Then review your responses to the previous learning activities and rank these factors in order of *your view* about their value to you as a supervisor in motivating your work team. After you have ranked the factors, identify the ones that you can control or influence as motivational strategies.

____ **Recognition:** Receiving recognition from peers, supervisors, and/or subordinates for good work.

____ **Sense of achievement:** Positive feelings associated with completing a job, finding solutions to different problems, or seeing the results of work.

____ **Advancement:** The opportunity to advance in the organization as a direct result of accomplishments and demonstrated skills and ability.

____ **Status:** Getting various "perks" such as a nice office/work space, a reserved parking space, or knowing that people look to you for direction.

____ **Pay:** A good salary.

____ **Supervision:** Working for someone who is competent, looks out for the welfare of subordinates, and that you respect.

____ **Job itself:** Having a job that is interesting and challenging and provides variety and autonomy.

____ **Job security:** Feeling confident that you will continue to have a job/place in the organization over the long term.

____ **Coworkers:** Working with people who are friendly, helpful, and competent.

____ **Personal development:** Getting the opportunity to develop and refine your knowledge, skills, and abilities that may lead to advancement.

____ **Fringe benefits:** A fringe benefits package that meets your needs and those of your family.

____ **Working conditions:** Working in a safe, secure, healthy, and attractive place.

Use this list as a guide to strategies for motivating your team. You might consider using the same list with your staff to find out whether your priorities match those of your employees.

TAKING IT FORWARD

Review the checklist on page 225 of *Effective Supervisory Practices* and the review questions and activities you have worked on for this lesson. Select *one* area related to motivation that you want to focus on and identify *three actions* you will take immediately to improve your effectiveness in motivating your employees. After you have worked on these actions for at least one month, document what happened and what you have learned that can help you be more successful as a supervisor when it comes to energizing, inspiring, and motivating your employees.

Unit V:

MANAGING THE WORKPLACE ENVIRONMENT

5

The lessons in this unit focus on your role in creating a work environment that supports high performance and positive results. The unit provides information and tools for helping you create a dynamic, positive, and productive workplace environment.

Lesson 13: Leading Change

Lesson 14: Ensuring a Harassment-Free and Respectful Workplace

Lesson 15: Workplace Safety, Security, and Wellness

Lesson 13:
LEADING CHANGE

Lesson objective:
To maximize knowledge of and supervisory skill in leading change processes to improve effectiveness.

Reading assignment:
Effective Supervisory Practices Fifth Edition, Chapter 13: Leading Change

Lesson outcomes:
When you finish this lesson, you should

- Understand why an openness to change in policies, procedures, equipment, and more is important to work unit success
- Be familiar with strategies for assessing the potential benefits of work improvements and changes
- Know your role in introducing and leading necessary changes
- Be aware of the potential challenges of and obstacles to introducing changes in your work unit
- Know the three-step process for building commitment to change.

Lesson overview

This lesson is designed to increase your understanding of the value of organizational change and enhance your skill in introducing new approaches in your work unit from initial idea to long-term commitment. It explores how to deal with the range of emotions that often accompany the idea of change and provides activities to help you manage the change process.

Review questions

1. What types of changes might you consider in your work unit? What factors might lead you to consider making changes in your work unit?
2. What should you take into account when thinking through a change and its implications for your work unit?
3. What makes implementing change in a work unit difficult or stressful?

4. What is a "pilot project," and how might a pilot project be used when introducing a new idea or new approach to your team?
5. What questions should you ask yourself before launching a change process to fix a troublesome operation?
6. Identify the six stages that people move through in responding to change.
7. What is the difference between a commitment to change and compliance with an implemented change?
8. Describe the three steps of change leadership that will help you build commitment to a change among your team members. Based on your experience, what is the most important step to take to gain employee commitment?
9. What are the benefits of involving employees in the change process?
10. Have you ever been involved in a change process that didn't go well? What went wrong? What could have been done differently?
11. What are the three most important ideas you gained from reading this chapter that you believe will help you become a better supervisor?

Learning activities

Activity 13.1 Attitudes toward change

Read each of the following statements and indicate whether you agree (A) or disagree (D) with each, based on both your work for this lesson and your experience, by putting an A or D in the space preceding each statement.

_____ 1. Most employees don't like change.

_____ 2. Most organizational changes are designed to increase efficiency or productivity.

_____ 3. The best way to introduce change is to get it over all at once.

_____ 4. If employees are uncomfortable with change, they will tell their supervisors about it.

_____ 5. Most employees either reject or accept all changes, regardless of what the changes are.

____ 6. Asking employees to participate in the change process is likely to reduce their opposition to change.

____ 7. Many supervisors underestimate the amount of time needed to implement a change.

____ 8. An evaluation of how the change has affected the organization should be made after the change has been implemented.

____ 9. Many employees fear that change will result in lower salaries, demotions, or layoffs.

____ 10. When changes are ordered by top management, supervisors should wait until they have all the facts before talking to employees.

After completing your assessment of each statement, compare notes with other supervisors in your class to reach agreement on *agrees* and *disagrees*. Then discuss what these statements tell you about attitudes and obstacles to introducing change in your work unit. If you are not working in a class, meet with an experienced supervisor in your department or with your own direct supervisor to review the statements and get additional input on attitudes toward change. Lastly, you can use these ten statements as a discussion tool with your employees to get their ideas and reactions to change in the workplace to increase the likelihood of successful implementation of change.

Activity 13.2 Thinking through a change process

Think about a possible change in how your unit carries out its work that you might consider pursuing. Define that change as specifically as you can at this stage. Then use the questions on pages 229 to 231 of Chapter 13 in *Effective Supervisory Practices* to assess whether you are ready to pursue a change proposal and to assess the potential for success. What conclusions did you reach about your possible change idea after completing the assessment? What additional groundwork, research, or group discussion might be needed to produce a positive outcome from implementing the change?

Activity 13.3 **Practicing leading change**

Read the supervisory situation on page 244 of Chapter 13. Think about the information in each situation, your experience as a supervisor, and what you have learned in this lesson. Then answer the questions for each supervisory situation taking into account both the specifics of the situations and how they might apply to your local government.

TAKING IT FORWARD

Review the checklist on page 243 of *Effective Supervisory Practices* and the review questions and activities you have worked on for this lesson. Then identify up to *three improvements* you might want to consider in your work unit and use the guidelines in the chapter to guide you through considering a change process. After you have worked on this idea for at least one month, document what happened and what you have learned that can help you be more successful as a supervisor when it comes to leading a change process.

Lesson 14:
ENSURING A HARASSMENT-FREE AND RESPECTFUL WORKPLACE

Lesson objective:
To establish the importance of promoting a healthy and inclusive work environment.

Reading assignment:
Effective Supervisory Practices Fifth Edition, Chapter 14: Ensuring a Harassment-Free and Respectful Workplace

Lesson outcomes:
When you finish this lesson, you should

- Understand and be able to recognize discrimination, harassment, and disrespectful behavior in your workplace
- Be familiar with your organization's harassment policy
- Know how you should respond to discrimination and harassment situations and complaints
- Understand the opportunities and challenges of diverse workplaces.

Lesson overview

You play an important role in ensuring a harassment-free and respectful workplace. This lesson provides information about the legal foundation for carrying out that role and offers practical advice, action steps, and tools for promoting a work environment where employees value and respect each other.

Review questions

1. What are the definitions of and differences among discrimination, harassment, and disrespectful behavior?
2. Drawing on both the chapter and your personal experience, provide a list of the types of behaviors that are always prohibited in the workplace.
3. What are your most important roles as a supervisor in promoting a respectful workplace?
4. What are the primary components of an organization's harassment policy?
5. Identify and explain the major federal laws on discrimination and harassment.

6. What is a harassment or discrimination complaint? What are your three responsibilities when you become aware of behavior that is prohibited by the organization's harassment policy?
7. If you observe an employee behaving in a way that you believe violates the organization's harassment policy, what should you do? If the employee tells you he or she was just joking around, what should you do?
8. What is subtle sexual harassment?
9. What steps should you follow as a fact finder when dealing with a possible discrimination or harassment complaint?
10. What is an intervention? How do you carry out an effective intervention?
11. What is retaliation and how can you protect employees from retaliation?
12. What are the three most important ideas you gained from reading this chapter that you believe will help you become a better supervisor?

Learning activities

Activity 14.1 Understanding your organization's harassment policy

It is essential that you are familiar with your organization's harassment policy and complaint process so that you can carry out your supervisory responsibilities. This activity is designed to connect you to your organization's structure for ensuring a harassment-free workplace by becoming familiar with all relevant policies and procedures. If you haven't previously reviewed your organization's policies and procedures, get copies and review them carefully. Using the three components of a typical policy that are listed on page 250 of Chapter 14 in *Effective Supervisory Practices*, identify the specific types of behavior that are prohibited, what the policy says about your responsibilities as a supervisor in preventing workplace harassment, and the specific steps for filing and handling a complaint. As part of your review, identify any areas in the policy that aren't clear to you or on which you need additional guidance and either raise them in your class discussion or talk to your organization's human resources officer for clarification.

Activity 14.2 Raising employee awareness of prohibited behaviors

Making sure your employees understand the importance of and are committed to ensuring a harassment-free and respectful workplace is the best way to minimize problems and prevent complaints before they happen. Both the chapter and your organization's policies identify specific types of unwelcome and prohibited behaviors. Using the chapter, your organization's policy, and your personal experience, prepare an outline for a discussion you will have with your team to make them aware of their roles in ensuring a harassment-free and respectful workplace. Review your outline in class or with another supervisor and then decide if and when to hold the discussion. What concerns or reservations do you have, if any, about having this conversation? What can you do to overcome those concerns? Consider talking to your organization's human resources officer for guidance on how to ensure that employees are well informed about their roles and yours in ensuring a harassment-free workplace.

Activity 14.3 Carrying out an effective intervention

An intervention is an action step you take as a supervisor to clarify the organization's harassment policy, encourage open communication, and stop prohibited behavior. If you don't intervene to stop prohibited behavior that you see, hear, or read, you risk being disciplined for allowing a hostile work environment to exist. Using the eight steps on pages 258 to 259 in Chapter 14 and working with another supervisor in your class, carry out a practice intervention with an employee to tell an employee that having a screen saver of a naked person is inappropriate. Be sure to follow the steps in the chapter including preparing a brief summary of what information you would provide to the human resources department (Step 7) about your conversation and the outcome. Or, if you have a specific issue or problem that could be prohibited behavior, use the eight steps to prepare for an effective intervention by practicing the conversation with another supervisor.

Activity 14.4 **Practicing and ensuring a harassment-free and respectful workplace**

Read the four supervisory situations on pages 260 to 263 of Chapter 14. Think about the information in the situation, your experience as a supervisor, and what you have learned in this lesson. Then answer the questions for the supervisory situation taking into account both the specifics of the situations and how they might apply to your local government. After you have responded to the questions for each situation, compare your thoughts with the guidance provided for each situation. If your approach differs from the guidance, review and discuss what led to your differences of opinion.

TAKING IT FORWARD

Review the checklist on page 260 of *Effective Supervisory Practices* and the review questions and activities you have worked on for this lesson. Then select one specific area that you believe will have a positive impact on ensuring a harassment-free and respectful workplace, such as becoming more familiar with your responsibilities and your organization's policy, talking with your employees about their responsibilities and what constitutes unacceptable or prohibited behavior, or modeling respectful behavior. After you have worked on this positive action step for at least one month, document what happened and what you have learned that can help you be more successful as a supervisor in ensuring a harassment-free and respectful workplace.

Lesson 15:
WORKPLACE SAFETY, SECURITY, AND WELLNESS

Lesson objective:
To increase supervisory competence in creating a safe, secure, and healthy workplace.

Reading assignment:
Effective Supervisory Practices Fifth Edition, Chapter 15: Workplace Safety, Security, and Wellness

Lesson outcomes:
When you finish this lesson, you should

- Understand your role in ensuring workplace safety
- Be familiar with national organizations that are responsible for supporting workplace safety
- Know the general elements of an effective workplace safety program
- Understand the causes of workplace accidents in order to prevent them from happening
- Know your role in keeping your workplace secure
- Be familiar with the benefits of and approaches to a workplace wellness program.

Lesson overview

Creating a safe, secure, and healthy workplace is another aspect of your supervisory responsibilities. While the organization probably has a safety program in place, you are responsible for knowing the details of the plan and ensuring that your employees pay close attention to safety on the job. This lesson focuses on your role in workplace safety, security, and wellness to increase your skills, competence, and comfort in carrying out this responsibility.

Review questions

1. What are the primary impacts of work-related injuries and illnesses in the organization, your work unit, and the members of your team?
2. What is the mission of the Occupational Safety and Health Administration (OSHA), and how does it relate to safety in your work unit?
3. What are the key elements of an effective workplace safety program?

4. Given the type of work your unit is responsible for, what are the biggest risks to employee safety?
5. What are the four major causes of workplace accidents?
6. What is workplace *security* and how does it differ from workplace *safety*? What, if any, are the primary risks to security in your work unit?
7. What steps can you take as a supervisor to prevent workplace violence?
8. What are some benefits of a workplace health and wellness program?
9. What are the three most important ideas you gained from reading this chapter that you believe will help you become a better supervisor?

Learning activities

Activity 15.1 Assessing the workplace safety environment

The following questions can be used to help you assess the overall safety environment in your work unit and potential areas that need attention to ensure a safe workplace.

1. Are your employees motivated to be safety conscious? What encouragement, incentives, or rewards do you, as a supervisor, provide to those who pay close attention to safe practices?
2. Have you examined your rules, procedures, and rewards to eliminate any that might encourage unsafe practices (e.g., procedures that encourage speed over safety)?
3. Have you surveyed your team's work environment to identify potential safety risks?
4. Do you provide a comprehensive orientation for new employees about safety rules and regulations? Are new employees trained to use equipment correctly, effectively, and safely?
5. Have you reviewed your records for trends in injuries, accidents, and near accidents?
6. Have any of your employees collected workers' compensation during the past year? How much has your local government paid in workers' compensation?

7. Have any of your employees been unable to perform his or her job during the past year because of injuries? What has been the impact of inability to perform on work unit outcomes?
8. What types of accidents occur most often on your work team? Is there a pattern to these accidents? What can you learn from accident trends?
9. If there have been accidents over the past year, what are the most frequent causes? Human error? Mechanical or equipment problems? Other?
10. Do you inspect equipment regularly? Do you have a regular schedule for routine maintenance to keep equipment in proper working order?
11. Is any of the equipment used by your team old or in poor condition? Does it need to be repaired or replaced? Does your organization have a regular schedule for replacing equipment? Is it followed?
12. Are any of the materials used by your team heavy, sharp, or toxic? Are employees adequately trained in handling these materials?

Based on your personal review of these questions, identify areas that you believe need more focus and attention. You can discuss your findings with others in your class and with your employees to identify specific action areas to improve safety in your work unit.

Activity 15.2 **Encouraging good safety habits**

Good safety habits begin with a leadership commitment to safety. If you expect your employees to comply with established safety guidelines, you must constantly demonstrate that you believe in workplace safety and that you live it. Drawing on the information in the *Effective Supervisory Practices* chapter, your personal experience, and guidelines for workplace safety in your local government, prepare a list of principles and actions you already take regularly or that you plan to take based on this course to demonstrate to your employees that you believe in workplace safety and that you live it.

Activity 15.3 Practicing workplace safety, security, and wellness

Read the three supervisory situations on pages 277 to 278 of Chapter 15. Think about the information in the situation, your experience as a supervisor, and what you have learned in this lesson. Then answer the questions for the supervisory situation taking into account both the specifics of the situations and how they might apply to your local government.

TAKING IT FORWARD

Review the checklist on page 277 of *Effective Supervisory Practices* and the review questions and activities you have worked on for this lesson. Then select one specific area that you believe will have a positive impact on workplace safety, security, and wellness in your work unit, drawing particularly on your safety assessment in Activity 15.1. After you have worked on this positive action step for at least one month, document what happened and what you have learned that can help you be more successful as a supervisor in ensuring safety, security, and wellness in your work unit.

6

Unit VI:

SERVING THE PUBLIC

This unit focuses on the essential role all local government employees play in serving the public by providing quality customer service. The final lesson based on the book provides a framework for raising awareness and reinforcing the importance of quality customer service.

Lesson 16: Quality Customer Service

Lesson 16:
QUALITY CUSTOMER SERVICE

Lesson objective:

To increase attention to and skill in ensuring the best possible service to both internal and external customers.

Reading assignment:

Effective Supervisory Practices Fifth Edition, Chapter 16: Quality Customer Service

Lesson outcomes:

When you finish this lesson, you should

- Know who your customers are
- Be committed to ensuring exceptional customer service
- Understand your role in motivating, guiding, and supporting your employees in delivering exceptional customer service
- Know the factors that are essential to providing high-quality customer service.

Lesson overview

This lesson focuses on building your awareness of and skill in ensuring that your employees know the importance of providing quality customer service. It provides concepts, tools, and resources to help you define who your customers are, understand their expectations, and create an environment where exceptional customer service is a daily priority.

Review questions

1. Who are your work unit's customers? Make a list of both external and internal customers and what you believe these customers want, need, and expect from your department or division.
2. Chapter 16 in *Effective Supervisory Practices* makes this observation on page 285: "All local government employees are ambassadors who represent their government to its citizens." How do you and your employees carry out their role as ambassadors who represent the government to its citizens? What specific actions do you and your employees take as ambassadors?

3. What are the key factors that are essential to providing high-quality customer service? Which of the factors listed on pages 286 to 291 of Chapter 16 are most important to your work unit?
4. What steps can you take to deal with difficult customers?
5. What tools can be used to measure customer service? What is your role in creating tools to measure customer service?
6. How do your customers feel about the local government and the work of your team? What evidence do you have to support your assessment of customer attitudes toward the local government and your team's work?
7. What are the three most important ideas you gained from reading this chapter that you believe will help you become a better supervisor?

Learning activities

Activity 16.1 Assessing professionalism and service ethic

A variety of factors contribute to professionalism and a commitment to service. You can use the following questions to assess your professionalism and service ethic and that of your unit.

1. Am I dressed appropriately for the tasks I am expected to perform today?
2. Does my work unit have a dress code? If not, should it?
3. Do I communicate pride in my work and in my government?
4. Do I understand my agency's mission and priorities, and can I articulate them to others?
5. Do I have the expertise and resources to perform my work to the level expected of me? If not, where can I get what is needed?
6. Does my team share a commitment to customer service?
7. Are we following through on the commitments we have made to others?
8. Is our work area clear and well organized? Is my desk or individual work area neat?
9. When someone approaches me, do I always acknowledge that person's presence, either by speaking or nodding? Do I do this even when I am involved in some other task or cannot talk to the person immediately?

10. Is the culture in our workplace service-oriented? Are team members engaged and happy to be at work?

After reviewing these questions personally, focus on any to which you responded *no*, and identify action steps you can take to improve your professionalism and service ethic. Then consider reviewing the questions with members of your team to develop a shared commitment to professionalism and service.

Activity 16.2 **Providing exceptional customer service**

Pages 286 to 291 of Chapter 16 in *Effective Supervisory Practices* identify factors that are essential to providing high-quality customer service. Review the factors carefully and then rate your team's overall effectiveness in providing exceptional customer service by assigning a number to how well they handle each factor: 3 (always), 2 (sometimes), 1 (rarely/never).

1. Accessible and responsive to all customers
2. Neat and professional work environment
3. Courteous to all customers
4. A customer-driven culture
5. Pride in team appearance
6. Effective communication and engagement with customers
7. Willingness to listen to customer needs, expectations, problems, and complaints
8. Demonstrated empathy in dealing with angry or frustrated customers
9. Demonstrated credibility and competence in answering questions and dealing with service requests
10. Commitment to technology to support customer service
11. Demonstrated ownership of issues and questions from customers.

Based on your ratings, identify your unit's strengths and weaknesses and develop a list of action steps that will move all ratings to "always" (3) within a defined time frame.

Activity 16.3 Practicing quality customer service

Read the supervisory situation on pages 296 to 297 of Chapter 16. Think about the information in the situation, your experience as a supervisor, and what you have learned in this lesson. Then answer the questions for the supervisory situation taking into account both the specifics of the situation and how they might apply to your local government.

TAKING IT FORWARD

Review the checklist on page 296 of *Effective Supervisory Practices* and the review questions and activities you have worked on for this lesson. Then select one specific area that you believe will have a positive impact on customer service in your work unit, drawing on the two assessments you completed in Activity 16.1 and Activity 16.2. After you have worked on this positive action step for at least one month, document what happened and what you have learned that can help you be more successful as a supervisor in ensuring that your unit is committed to exceptional customer service every day.

Unit VII:

BECOMING A SUCCESSFUL SUPERVISOR

7

This unit focuses on you and what you have accomplished in your transition from employee to supervisor to leader. This final lesson provides a framework for action planning to help you summarize what you have learned during this course and develop action strategies for applying what you have learned on the job.

Lesson 17: Action Planning

Lesson 17:
ACTION PLANNING

Lesson objective:
To summarize key learning points and identify action steps for future growth as a supervisor.

Reading assignment:

- Review ***Effective Supervisory Practices*** Fifth Edition, Chapter 1: Roles of a Supervisor
- Review selected chapters of special interest
- Review personal notes focusing particularly on your "Taking It Forward" commitments.

Lesson outcomes:
When you finish this lesson, you should

- Know what you got out of the course and what you plan to do next to continue your learning
- Be more comfortable with your roles as a supervisor and more confident in your supervisory skills
- Have more answers to the questions you had when you started this course.

Lesson overview

This lesson is designed to help you convert what you have learned during this course into a personal action plan to improve your effectiveness as a supervisor. To prepare for this lesson, you should review Chapter 1 in *Effective Supervisory Practices* along with any other chapters that were particularly interesting, relevant to your job, or challenging for you. You should also do some reflection about your role as a supervisor and what you have learned that you believe will make you a better supervisor going forward.

Learning activities

Activity 17.1 Reassessing your supervisory skills

Review the seven questions that you used in Activity 1.2 on page 5 of this study guide to assess your supervisory skills at the start of this course and your responses to those questions. Then use those questions again to assess your supervisory skills as you finish the course.

Activity 17.2 Assessing progress on becoming a successful supervisor

Revisit the graphic on page 13 of Chapter 1 in *Effective Supervisory Practices* and your assessment of your current skill level in each of the six characteristics of a successful supervisor:

1. Communication skills
2. Loyalty
3. Positive attitude
4. Desire for the job
5. Ability to delegate
6. Fairness.

Would you rate yourself any differently at the conclusion of the course and the actions you have taken forward to apply skills learned in the classroom back on the job? At the conclusion of this course, which characteristic seems most important to you now in your supervisory development? Is it the same characteristic that you selected at the beginning of this course? If not, what led you to choose a different characteristic?

Activity 17.3 Reviewing learning objectives

Review the personal learning objectives you set for Activity 1.6 at the beginning of this course. Then think about and respond to the following questions:

1. How do you feel about the course now that you have completed all the lessons?
2. Identify three specific ways you have used what you learned during the lessons on the job.
3. What is the best thing that happened to you as a supervisor while working on the course?
4. Are you able to answer the three questions that you wanted to answer about your job as a supervisor when you finished the course?

Then review the five learning objectives you prepared at the start of the course and assess whether you feel equipped to do what you "hoped" you would be able to do when you finished the course.

Activity 17.4 Action plan

Use the following two worksheets to identify specific *supervisory skills* that you want to continue to work on based on your experience in this course and *specific action strategies* you want to implement in your work unit to improve its overall effectiveness. Your skill targets may be built around areas that you identified as weaknesses or that seem particularly important in your supervisory role right now. Examples of specific action strategies include dealing with a specific employee performance or behavior problem, introducing a new approach to carrying out your unit's work, raising awareness among your employees about ethics, or developing a plan to improve workplace safety.

Supervisory skills worksheet

Note to supervisors: Make separate worksheets for each skill on which you want to focus.

1. Specific supervisory skill that I would like to improve

2. Why this skill is important to my work group

3. Specific steps I will take to develop this skill further

4. How I will measure/assess progress on improving this skill

5. Other people who can contribute to my further developing this skill

6. Time frame for showing progress on developing this skill

Action strategies worksheet

Note to supervisors: Make separate worksheets for each issue on which you want to focus.

1. Specific issue, problem, or challenge that I would like to address in my work unit to improve overall effectiveness

2. Outcome or outcomes I hope to achieve by addressing this issue, problem, or challenge

3. Specific steps I will take to initiate work on this issue, problem, or challenge

4. How I will measure/assess progress on achieving the outcomes

5. Other people who can contribute to addressing this issue, problem, or challenge

6. Time frame for showing progress on addressing this issue, problem, or challenge

---